ESCAPE ROOM PUZZLES
ATTACK OF THE MEGA BUGS

KINGFISHER
LONDON & NEW YORK

Copyright © Macmillan Publishers
International Ltd 2023
Published in the United States by Kingfisher
120 Broadway, New York, NY 10271
Kingfisher is a division of Macmillan Children's
Books, London

ISBN 978-0-7534-7883-7

Distributed in the U.S. and Canada by
Macmillan, 120 Broadway, New York, NY
10271

EU representative: Macmillan Publishers
Ireland Ltd, 1st Floor, The Liffey Trust Centre,
117-126 Sheriff Street Upper, Dublin 1, D01
YC43.

Library of Congress Cataloging-in-Publication
data has been applied for.

Written, designed and illustrated
by Dynamo Limited

Kingfisher books are available for special
promotions and premiums. For details
contact:
Special Markets Department, Macmillan, 120
Broadway, New York, NY 10271.

For more information, please visit
www.kingfisherbooks.com.

Printed in China
9 8 7 6 5 4 3 2 1
1TR/0323/WKT/UG/128MA

ESCAPE ROOM PUZZLES
ATTACK OF THE MEGA BUGS

KINGFISHER
LONDON & NEW YORK

CONTENTS

MEET THE TEAM!   6

HELLO!   7

ROOM ONE:
THE WELCOME TOUR   8

SANCTUARY SPOTTING   10

CHEWED UP   12

BACK TO CAMP   14

ROOM TWO:
THE TREEHOUSE   16

TENT TROUBLE   18

NIGHTTIME NASTIES   20

TREEHOUSE   22

MARKS IN THE BARK   24

ROOM THREE:
THE LAB   26

BUG BURST-OUT   28

BEELINE   30

SPECIMEN STUDIES   **32**

SUDOKU   **34**

FEAST FOR BEASTS   **36**

ROOM FOUR:
THE DESERT ZONE   **38**

DRINK UP   **40**

PICK A PATH   **42**

MEERKAT CODE   **44**

BIRD'S EYE VIEW   **46**

ROOM FIVE:
THE TROPIC ZONE   **48**

SYMMETRY IN STRIPES   **50**

ENCLOSURE BUILD   **52**

POTENT PICKLE   **54**

SNEAKY SLOTH   **56**

BUG-EYED   **58**

ROUND-UP   **60**

ANSWERS   **62**

MEET THE TEAM!

Hey! I'm Kiran.

Ethan here!

NAME: Kiran

STRENGTHS: Leader and organizer

FUN FACT: Loves extreme sports–especially rock climbing

NAME: Ethan

STRENGTHS: Math and science genius

FUN FACT: Amazing memory for facts and always wins any quiz

Hello! Zane's the name.

Hi!

NAME: Zane

STRENGTHS: Creative and thinks outside the box

FUN FACT: Loves art and takes his trusty sketchbook wherever he goes

NAME: Cassia

STRENGTHS: Technology pro

FUN FACT: Queen of gadgets and invents her own apps

HELLO!

Kiran, Ethan, Zane, and Cassia are all set for another adventure. This time, the gang are camping in the grounds of an animal sanctuary to study the declining animal population.

The park has seen an influx of mysterious and invasive bugs that are affecting the sanctuary's plants and the animals that eat them. The mysterious part is that nobody can trace the bug species, and nobody knows where they're coming from!

Kiran loves nature—especially creepy crawlies, so she's read all about the sanctuary and its unwelcome swarm of bugs. When their teacher broke the news that they were going on a school trip to this exact sanctuary, she was ecstatic. There's only one thing on Kiran's mind, and that's solving the mystery of the invasive insects.

WHAT YOU KNOW:

🐜 The invasive bugs have never been seen anywhere before.

🐜 They're affecting the other animals and plants in the sanctuary.

🐜 None of the rangers have been able to solve the issue.

YOUR MISSION:
To find the source of the invasive critters and stop them before any more damage is done. It's important to tackle this problem head on and prevent them from escaping into the outside world. Who knows what could happen then!

Don't forget!

You must find these six bugs that are hidden throughout the challenges.

ROOM ONE: THE WELCOME TOUR

The teacher leads you all into the grand entrance of the animal sanctuary. It's everything Zane, Ethan, Cassia, and Kiran had imagined it would be. No wonder it's world-famous! The impressive sanctuary is filled with vast, green enclosures holding every animal imaginable, from reptiles to zebras and giraffes. The class are greeted by a park ranger and some of the other staff who take care of the sanctuary.

Kiran eagerly waits for one of them to talk about the invasive bugs, but nobody mentions it. Before they know it, the ranger is showing them around their camp. The last thing on Kiran's mind is sleep, so she decides to volunteer the gang to help the park ranger. You never know, it might be a chance to spot some extra clues that will help the team solve the mystery.

SANCTUARY SPOTTING

Kiran and Ethan are helping the park ranger monitor the different species in the animal sanctuary. Can you find each animal in the enclosure?

Tick off each animal when you spot it.

CHEWED UP

Luckily the giraffe spits out the scrap of paper, but it's all wet and there are bits missing. You need to figure out a way to read that all-important passcode, or you'll be sleeping in one of the enclosures! Can you put it back together?

This must be the first part!

We've just got to match up the shapes.

G

06

ANIMAL FACT

With their extra-long legs and neck, giraffes are the tallest animals in the world. Males are around 18 feet—that's three times taller than a human!

Hint

Think about the sounds you hear in the wild.

O   RG LO   WL

Write out the passcode here:

Solved it!

You've successfully retrieved the passcode. What's up next?

BACK TO CAMP

Kiran was sure she'd have no trouble remembering the way back to camp, but she's gone blank. Luckily, Cassia has been tracking their movements all day with her app. But when she tries to use the navigation tool, the tablet screen fills with arrows. Follow the arrows to find your way across the animal sanctuary.

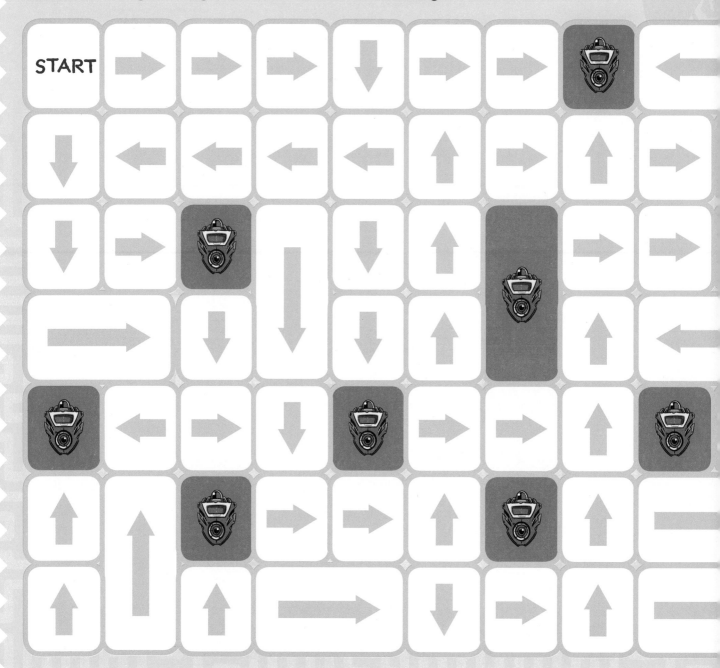

Be sure to dodge the red squares! Walk through those, and you'll activate the alarms.

FINISH

You spot an unusual bug, and Cassia scans it into her phone.

Breezed by

Well, that was impressive work! All that's left to do is settle down for some nocturnal wildlife watching.

ROOM TWO:
THE TREEHOUSE

Excellent job, team! You've helped monitor the animal species in the sanctuary, retrieved an important code from a giraffe, and managed to find your way back to camp . . . and it's only day one! But most importantly, you've had your first sighting of the menacing bugs. After making some quick sketches of the bugs, Zane suggests keeping watch after dark. If you're going to put a stop to the invasive critters once and for all, you must know as much about them as possible.

Before you can get going, you're going to need a place to keep all your belongings and get some rest. You've been allocated a tent, so now you just need to find it. The team steps into the camp zone and are faced with tent after tent. Your first task is to work out which one is yours.

TENT TROUBLE

The park warden has allocated the team two tents to sleep in, but which ones are they? The only instruction she has given is: "Find the two triangles that have identically matching symbols on them." Just then Cassia's tablet beeps, and a strange diagram appears on her screen.

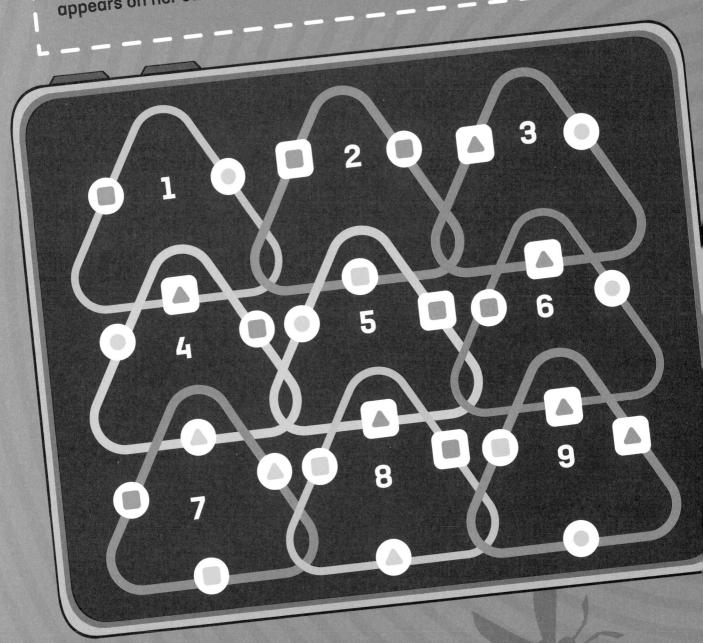

We're looking for matching symbols.

Make sure the symbols are in the same colors and places!

Aced it!

Inside the triangles are two tents with your names on them. You wander inside and set up your beds. No time to hang around though, you need to start investigating.

NIGHTTIME NASTIES

As darkness falls, the gang sneak out armed with all the supplies they'll need for a night of bug spotting. You must creep through the park while dodging the security cameras. Remember you can't backtrack or cross your own path.

START HERE

🐾 ANIMAL FACT

A group of owls is called a parliament. That might be because owls are considered wise and intelligent.

EXIT HERE

CHALLENGE RATING

Great moves

You make it through the park without being caught on camera. And you seem to have spotted where the bugs are coming from, too!

TREEHOUSE

You follow the trail of bugs, and it takes you to what looks like a treehouse. Just then you catch sight of the park ranger leaving the treehouse and locking the door behind her. Can you work out the door code so you can follow the bug trail inside the treehouse?

What's she doing in there at this time of night?

We need to do some digging!

Write the missing numbers in the triangles so that each side adds up to nine.

Make sure you don't repeat any numbers!

1

3

2

Practice some combinations here!

Nice going!

The door swings open. Into the treehouse you go . . .

MARKS IN THE BARK

Kiran leads the way into the treehouse. In the center is an enormous trunk. Zane locates a circle carved into it that looks like an opening. Cassia scans the trunk into her tablet, and three images of bark appear on the screen. You must select the section of bark that fits inside the circle. Ready, set . . . go!

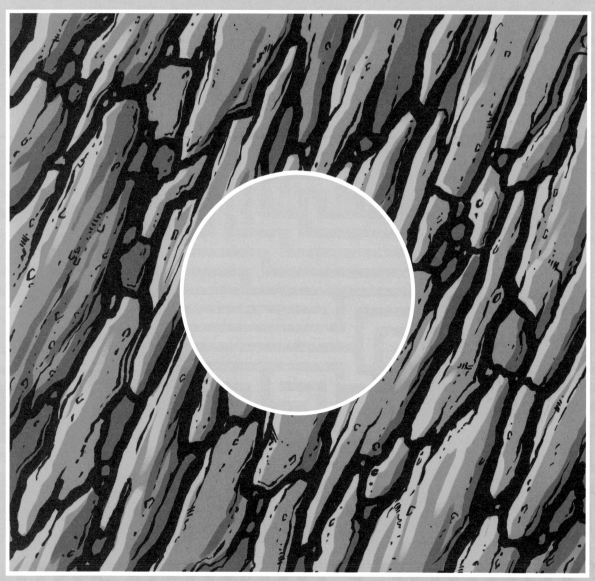

1

We need to match up the markings.

2

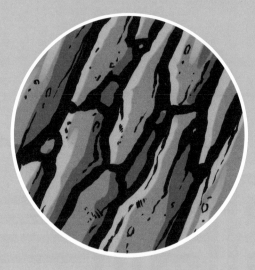

3

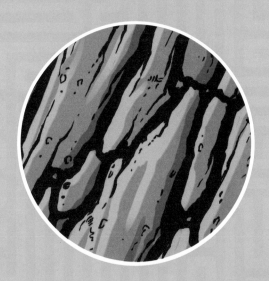

You're in!

You select the correct image, and the tree trunk creaks open.

ROOM THREE:
THE LAB

You all follow Kiran into another area of the treehouse, hoping to find the way out. But instead you soon come to a door that's been wedged open. There's a sign on it saying "The Lab: Keep Out" but there's no time to follow the rules—you've got an animal sanctuary to save!

Inside the lab, the sound of humming and buzzing makes it almost too hard to think. The insects are in here, and not just a few of them either. In fact, when you turn on the light, the room is filled with tanks from floor to ceiling. Each one has a different type of critter inside. Taped to each box is a label with scribbled handwriting on it. It looks like the park ranger has been cross-breeding bugs in this lab, and things have gotten seriously out of hand.

BUG BURST-OUT

Before you actually do any investigating, a swarm of bugs bursts out and fills the treehouse. Can you spot the bugs that match Zane's sketches exactly?

Wow! It's worse than I thought.

Good eye

You've identified the bugs that match Zane's sketch book. You have also identified just how many mutations of the bugs there really are.

BEELINE

The bugs are desperately trying to escape the lab! Everyone whips out a net from their rucksacks and tries to catch the insects. Follow the paths to see who catches the most bugs.

Kiran

Zane

Cassia

Ethan

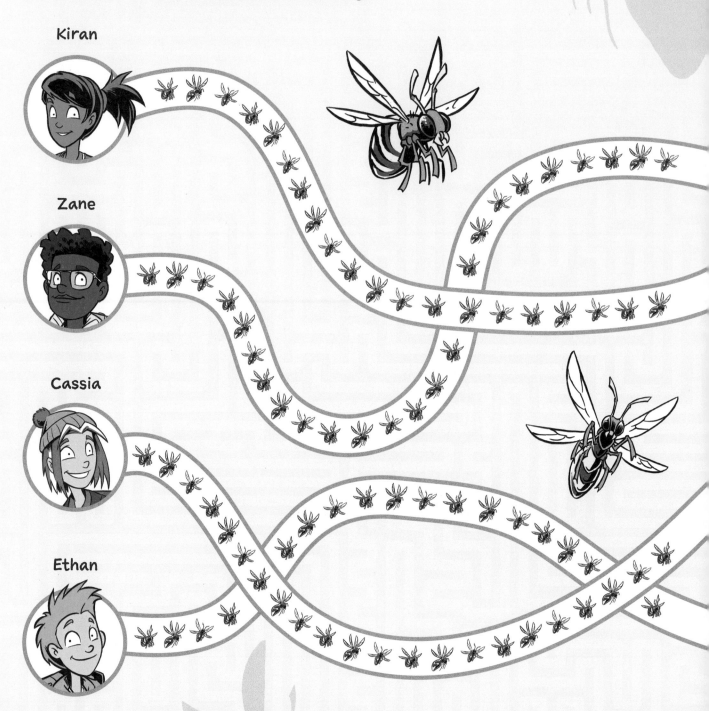

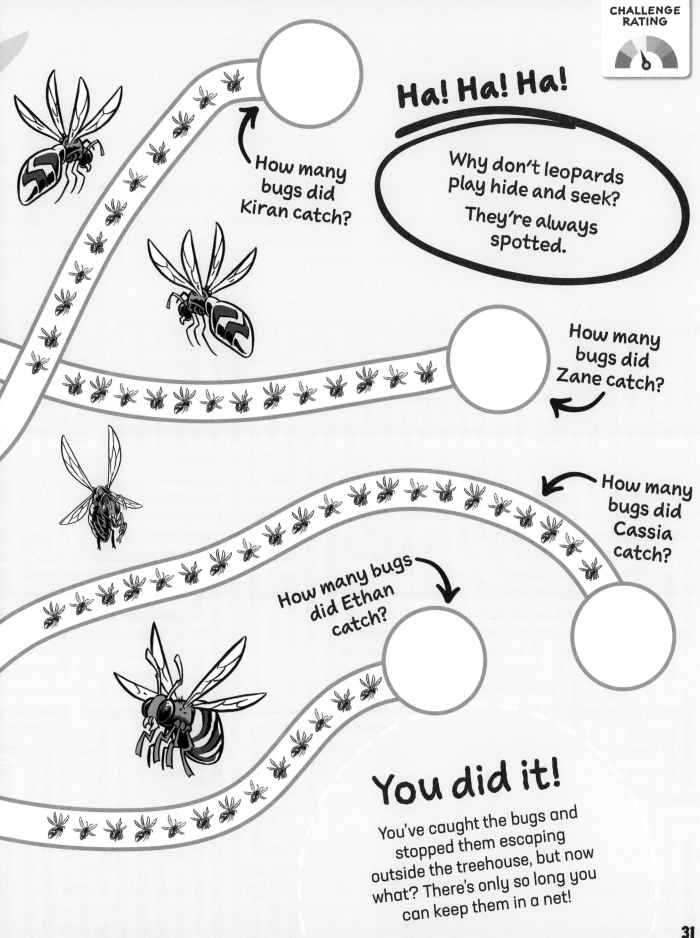

How many bugs did Kiran catch?

Ha! Ha! Ha!

Why don't leopards play hide and seek? They're always spotted.

How many bugs did Zane catch?

How many bugs did Cassia catch?

How many bugs did Ethan catch?

You did it!

You've caught the bugs and stopped them escaping outside the treehouse, but now what? There's only so long you can keep them in a net!

SPECIMEN STUDIES

Kiran finds some insect boxes on a shelf, and they carefully pop the insects inside them. She can't wait to take a better look at them all. Can you find the odd one out in each container?

They're so beautiful!

①

②

③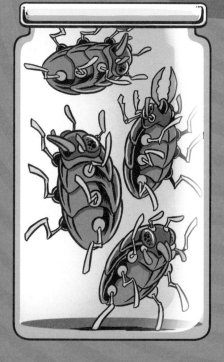

CHALLENGE RATING

4

5

6

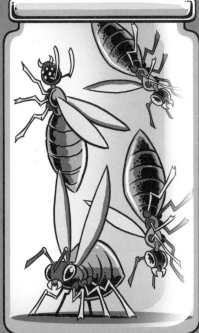

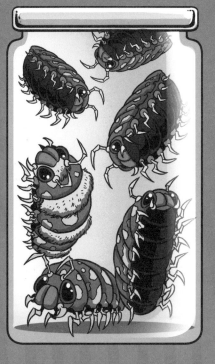

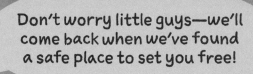

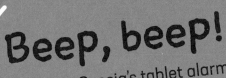

Don't worry little guys—we'll come back when we've found a safe place to set you free!

Beep, beep!

Just then Cassia's tablet alarm goes off. When she looks at the screen, all she can see is sudoku grids. It's your next task!

33

SUDOKU

Let's hope this sudoku screen will help you figure a way out of this treehouse. If you're locked in here much longer, someone is bound to find out you've been snooping. Complete the grids using the images at the bottom of the page.

| 1 | 2 | 3 | 4 | 5 | 6 |

Ha! Ha! Ha!

What did the tree wear to the pool party?
Trunks

Remember that each number should only appear once in each column, row and box of six.

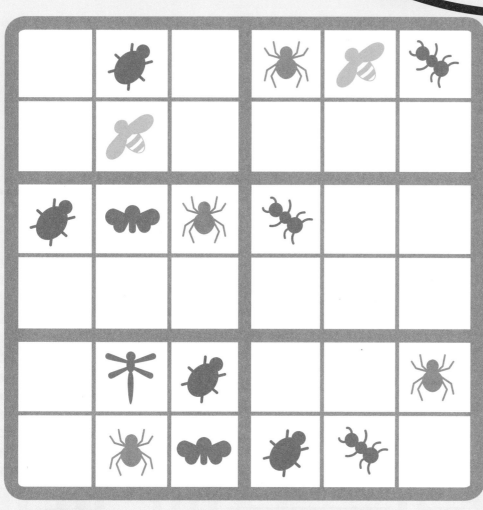

You're free!

A door on the other side of the treehouse opens, but where will it take you? Kiran leads the way down the ramp.

FEAST FOR BEASTS

You step out into the early morning sunshine, and the first thing you come across is an abandoned jeep covered in pesky weeds. You've got to get back to your tents before the teacher notices you are gone. Zane suddenly recognizes the jeep—it's the same one that was parked at the entrance when they arrived at the sanctuary. Can you spot the 10 differences between the two pictures?

We better get back to our tents before the teacher notices.

Yes, but look. The bugs are eating the weeds.

Chomp, chomp!

Cassia suddenly realizes how many bugs are chomping through the troublesome weeds. Maybe these weird bugs aren't that bad after all!

ROOM FOUR:
THE DESERT ZONE

Before the gang moves on, Cassia remembers an app that identifies plant species. She quickly scans the strange-looking weed to see if it registers. Success! The app describes it as a weed that can destroy other plant life and even buildings or solid structures (just like that jeep!) if left to grow wild. So if the bugs like this particular weed, they need to use that to their advantage before the weeds completely take over the animal sanctuary. But how will they do that without the bugs destroying everything else at the same time?

Just beyond the jeep is the gate into the sanctuary's desert zone. You can't go back the way you came because that means getting through the locked treehouse, so your only option is to enter the desert. This ground-breaking animal sanctuary is the first of its kind to cleverly manipulate the environment to mimic the desert. So the conditions inside this zone are as close to the real deal as you can get! Let's hope you discover some clues . . .

DRINK UP

Right at the entrance of the desert zone is a watering station. Rule number one in the desert—you need to stay hydrated! The only thing is: you need to work out the code to retrieve the water. Your task is to connect up the dots to reveal the number in each square. The key is to only connect up the numbers that are multiples of three.

Remember, you must go from smallest to biggest.

We need to remember our times tables!

40

③

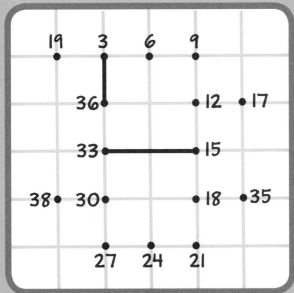

19   3   6   9

36•   •12 •17

33———————15

38• 30•   •18 •35

27   24   21

④

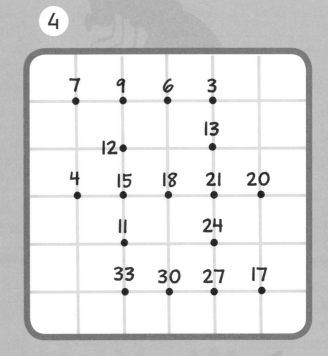

7   9   6   3

13

12•

4   15   18   21   20

11   24

33   30   27   17

Write your combination here.

Thirst quenched

Now you've got your water, you wander through the gates. A hot breeze escapes and blows over you all. Into the desert you go!

PICK A PATH

Suddenly the path you've been walking splits. Which side should you choose? Ethan notices some shapes painted on the ground next to a pair of dice. You must roll a certain color and number to complete the sequence below.

Look carefully at the sequence. Can you figure out what comes next?

Which one of these is correct?

Right, team! We've got this.

I can't wait to get in there.

Ha! Ha! Ha!

What type of bird is always on a construction site?

A crane

You did it!

Kiran draws the missing dice, and an arrow appears. It's leading you toward the meerkat enclosure.

MEERKAT CODE

The meerkats can sense that something is not right and are all on high alert. How are you going to get to the other side without spooking them? Not only that, but the door leading out seems to be locked with a keypad needing a 12-digit code. Zane finds a map and turns it over to reveal notes left by the park ranger.

It seems the coordinates of the holes that the meerkats don't use are a clue to the 12-digit code.

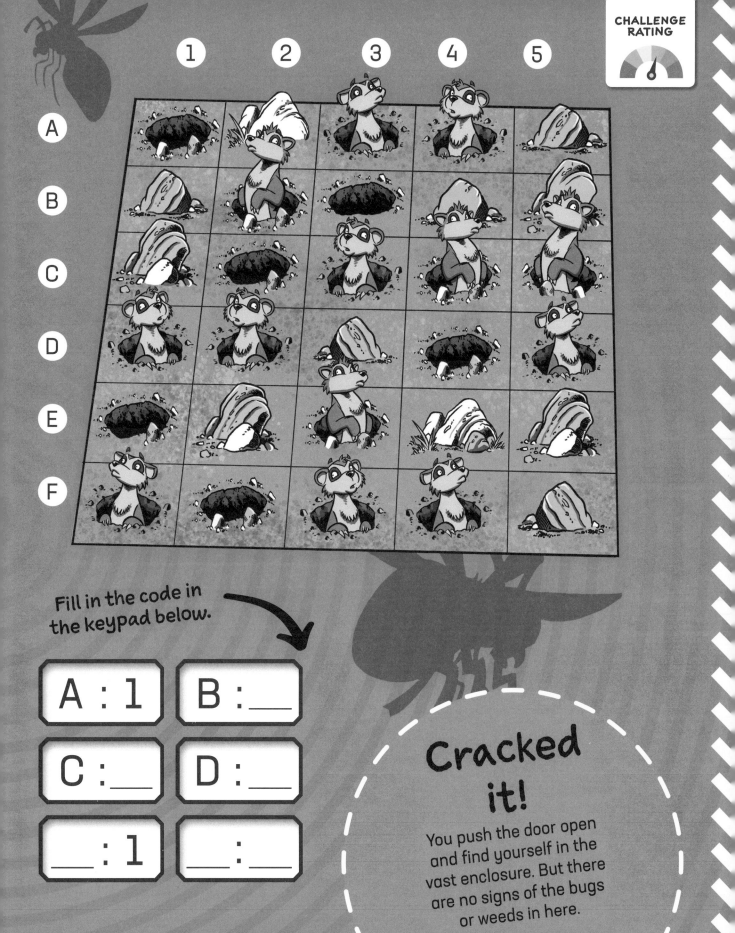

Fill in the code in the keypad below.

A : 1   B :__

C :__   D :__

__ : 1   __ :__

Cracked it!

You push the door open and find yourself in the vast enclosure. But there are no signs of the bugs or weeds in here.

BIRD'S-EYE VIEW

The severe lack of bugs around here suggests that this environment is not right for them. Perhaps it's too dry. What's the opposite of the dry desert? The humid tropics of course! Fallen trees are blocking the way into the tropics, so you're going to have to go around them! Follow the instructions and use the map to find the tropic zone.

Directions

Step 1: Travel 1 square south.

Step 2: Travel 8 squares west.

Step 3: Travel 3 squares north.

Step 4: Travel 1 square east.

Step 5: Travel 1 square north.

Step 6: Travel 7 squares east.

Check your directions with this compass!

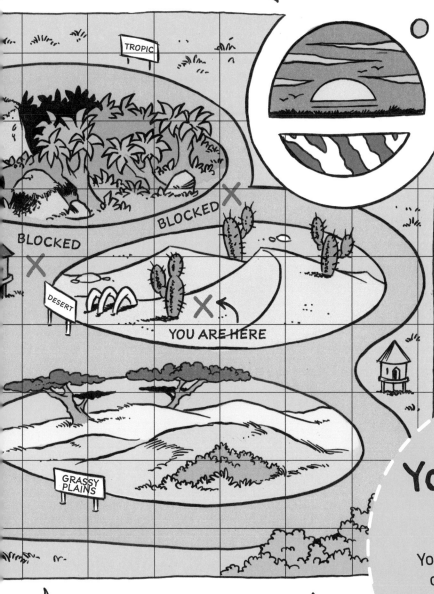

You've been caught!

You enter the tropic zone and come face to face with the park ranger. Uh oh!

ROOM FIVE:
THE TROPIC ZONE

There's no use trying to hide what you're up to from the park ranger now. So Cassia decides to own up. The ranger looks shocked when she discovers that the gang knows all about her secret treehouse and the weird bugs. She tells them that she'd cross-bred two critters, and the result was so beautiful that she wanted to try more and things had . . . gotten out of hand. She'd kept it hidden for so many months!

When Kiran tells the park ranger about how the bugs LOVE a certain weed, her face lights up. Zane shows her a sketch of the weed. The park ranger explains how the tropic zone is becoming a wasteland since it is so overrun with the weeds. That gives the gang an idea.

Together you come up with a plan to build a giant enclosure in the tropic zone to keep the weeds and the bugs under control. The ranger heads back to her treehouse to collect something she's been working on while the rest of you head into the tropic zone.

SYMMETRY IN STRIPES

Inside the tropic zone you are faced with three paths, with a picture of a tiger above each one. So, which should you choose? Cassia's tablet pings, and a task appears. Find the mirror image of this tiger, and that is the path you should take.

Pay close attention to their stripes!

Look, the images of the tigers have been flipped.

1   2   3

This is tricky.

Off you go!

You set off down that path and soon reach the site of the out-of-control weeds. Time to get started on that enclosure!

ENCLOSURE BUILD

Time to build this bug-friendly enclosure! You must place the blocks so that there are no gaps—gaps mean escaping bugs. Finish the enclosure on the grid using the blocks below. Remember that blocks CANNOT be rotated to fit the space.

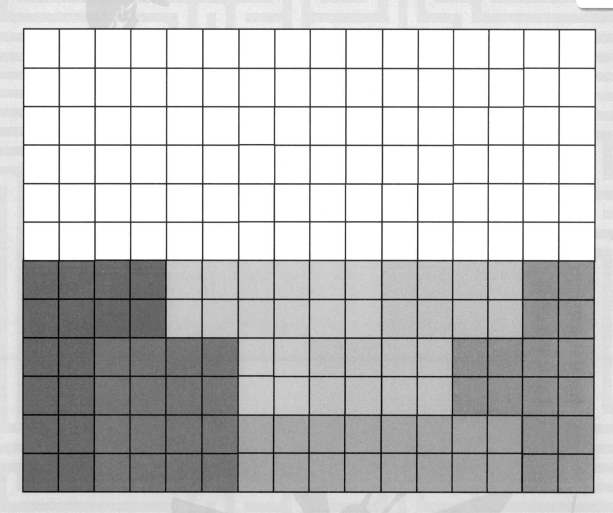

Ha! Ha! Ha!

Why are lions terrible storytellers?
They only have one tail.

Looking good

Now you just need to get the bugs inside. Just then you hear an engine revving, and the park ranger appears driving the weed-covered jeep.

POTENT PICKLE

The ranger has brought six bottles with her. One of the bottles contains a formula that attracts the invasive bugs, but she can't remember which one. Find the label that matches the one on her screen below.

1

2

3

4

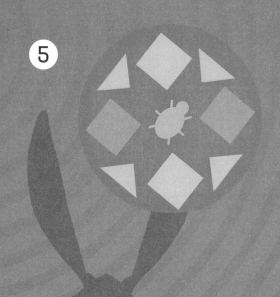

5

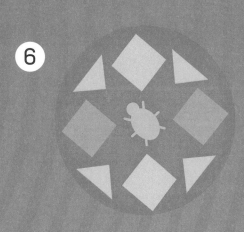

6

spray it!

Now you've got the spray, you can use it to lead the bugs toward the enclosure. Just spray it behind you as you drive!

SNEAKY SLOTH

Oh no, one of these sloths has taken the keys to the jeep! Luckily for you, sloths are not known for their speed. Unluckily for you, it has taken the keys deep into a mass of weeds. Follow the tangled weeds to see which sloth has taken them.

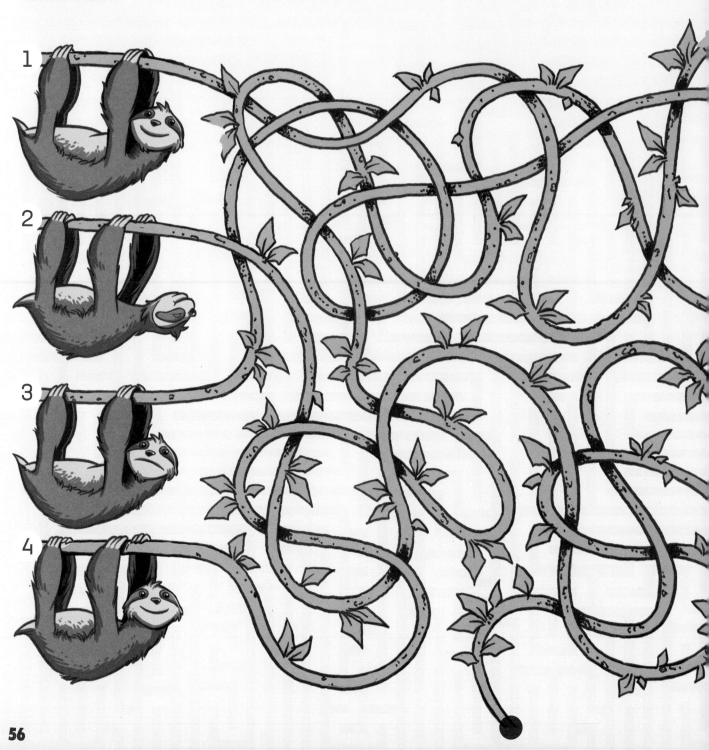

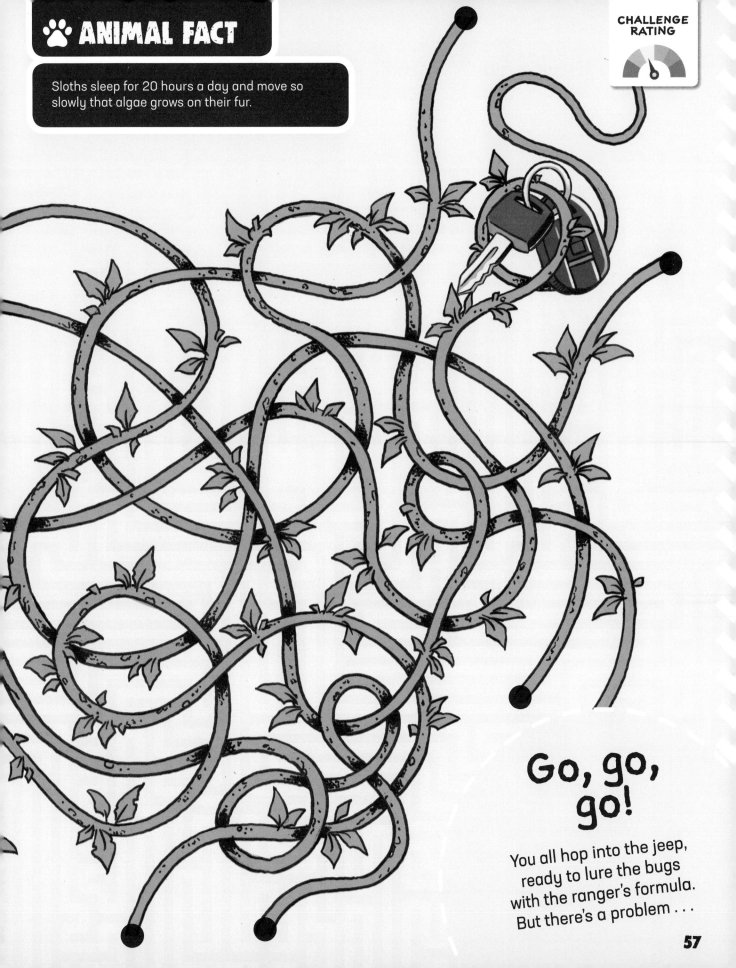

🐾 ANIMAL FACT

Sloths sleep for 20 hours a day and move so slowly that algae grows on their fur.

CHALLENGE RATING

Go, go, go!

You all hop into the jeep, ready to lure the bugs with the ranger's formula. But there's a problem . . .

BUG-EYED

The jeep's steering wheel is locked. You notice a picture of a bug on the dashboard. Cassia recognizes it from the ones she's been photographing. As she takes a photo of it, a cryptic puzzle appears. See the opposite page for a hint!

Your task is to put the bugs in order from least to most. Write the letters in the spaces.

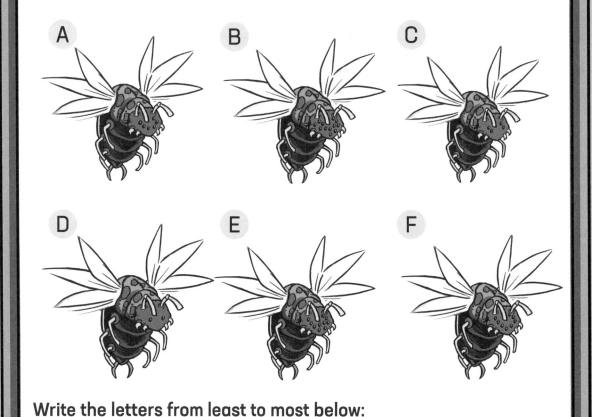

Write the letters from least to most below:

_____   _____   _____   _____   _____   _____

🐾 ANIMAL FACT

Fossils show that dragonflies have lived on Earth for 300 million years.

CHALLENGE RATING

Wow, this one has 10 eyes.

I don't get it. The bugs are all the same size!

Hive five!

Nothing gets past you guys! Are you ready for your next challenge?

ROUND-UP

Plenty of bugs have made their way to your fabulous enclosure, but you need to round up as many as possible—and fast. The ranger drives the jeep through each zone of the sanctuary (apart from the desert zone!) spraying the bug scent into the air. Lead them back to the enclosure you've built.

Cut through the center of each habitat.

START

You only have enough bug spray to pass each zone once.

CHALLENGE RATING

FINISH

YOU DID IT!

Impressive work. Together you've saved the sanctuary from being totally overrun with ghastly weeds and monster-sized bugs! Not only that—but you made it back to camp just in time for breakfast!

ANSWERS

PAGES 10-11
There are 6 bugs.

Pages 12-13
GROWLO6

Pages 14-15

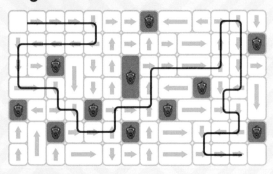

Pages 18-19
I and 6

Pages 20-21

Pages 22-23

Pages 24-25
2

Pages 28-29

Pages 30-31
Kiran	**31**
Zane	**37**
Cassia	**43** WINNER!
Ethan	**30**

Pages 32-33

Pages 34-35

Pages 36-37

Pages 40-41
1: **9**
2: **7**
3: **8**
4: **5**

Combination
9 7 8 5

Pages 42-43
2

Pages 44-45
A: **1**   B: **3**
C: **2**   D: **4**
E: **1**   F: **2**

Pages 46-47

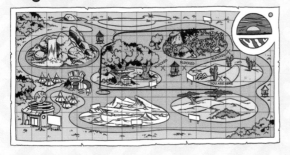

Pages 50-51
3

Pages 52-53

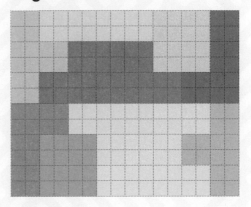

Pages 54-55
5

Pages 56-57
4

Pages 58-59
D C A F E B

Pages 60-61

SEE YOU ON THE NEXT ADVENTURE!

Color in the team!